NATIVE AMERICAN HISTORIES

THE SIOUX

BY MICHELLE LEVINE

CONSULTANT: HOLLY A. ANNIS
ITAZIPCO/MNICOUJOU LAKOTA, CHEYENNE RIVER SIOUX TRIBE

LERNER PUBLICATIONS COMPANY
MINNEAPOLIS

ABOUT THE COVER IMAGE: This shield was made by a person from the Oglala Sioux Tribe in South Dakota.

PHOTO ACKNOWLEDGMENTS:

The images in this book are used with permission of: © 2006 Harvard University, Peabody Museum, photo 16-20-10/86734, pp. 1, 3, 4, 14, 23, 30, 40; © Greg Ryan and Sally Beyer, p. 5; © Todd Strand/ Independent Picture Service, p. 7; Seth Eastman/Minnesota Historical Society, pp. 8, 20, 25; Agricultural Research Service, USDA, p. 10; Courtesy of the Division of Anthropology, American Museum of Natural History, pp. 11 [50/2909 AB], 18 [50.2/4473], 21 [50.2/4064, painting by Short Bull]; Photo courtesy of South Dakota State Historical Society—State Archives, p. 12; The New York Public Library/Art Resource, NY, p. 13; Museum of the American West Collection, Autry National Center, Los Angeles, p. 15; National Archives, pp. 16, 26, 32; Smithsonian American Art Museum, Washington, DC/Art Resource, NY, pp. 17, 19; © Arnaldo Magnani/Getty Images, p. 22; Brown Brothers, p. 24; Francis Davis Millet/Minnesota Historical Society, p. 27; Library of Congress, pp. 28, 34, 37; Minneapolis Public Library, p. 29; J. H. Anderson, courtesy Palace of the Governors (MNM/DCA), #144750, p. 33; Courtesy of the Autry National Center, Southwest Museum, Los Angeles. Photo #CT.1, p. 35; Cumberland County Historical Society, Carlisle, PA, p. 38; Smithsonian Institution National Anthropological Archives, Bureau of American Ethnology Collection, #55,659, p. 39; YMCA of the USA and Kautz Family Archives, p. 41: Photographic Archives, Harold B. Lee Library, Brigham Young University, P-MSS299, p. 42; AP/Wide World Photos, p. 43; © Cheryl Walsh Bellville, pp. 45, 46; Wisconsin Dells Visitors and Convention Bureau, p. 47; Photo by Stephanie Storer, courtesy of the Heritage Center at Red Cloud Indian School, Pine Ridge, South Dakota, p. 48; © A.A.M. Van der Heyden/Independent Picture Service, p. 49; © Tim Mosenfelder/Getty Images, p. 50.

Cover: Courtesy of the Division of Anthropology, American Museum of Natural History (50/2929).

Lerner Publications Company
A division of Lerner Publishing Group
241 First Avenue North
Minneapolis, MN 55401 U.S.A.

Website address: www.lernerbooks.com

Library of Congress Cataloging-in-Publication Data

Levine, Michelle.
   The Sioux / by Michelle Levine.
      p.   cm. — (Native American histories)
   Includes bibliographical references and index.
   ISBN-13: 978-0-8225-2864-7 (lib. bdg. : alk. paper)
   ISBN-10: 0-8225-2864-9 (lib. bdg. : alk. paper)
      1. Dakota Indians—History—Juvenile literature. 2. Dakota Indians—Social life and customs—Juvenile literature. I. Title. II. Series.
   E99.D1L48 2007
   978.004'975243—dc22   2005005655

Manufactured in the United States of America
1 2 3 4 5 6 – DP – 12 11 10 09 08 07

CONTENTS

CHAPTER 1

FROM WOODLANDS to PLAINS

THE SIOUX ARE AMERICAN INDIANS, or Native Americans. They have lived in the upper Midwest and the Great Plains of North America for hundreds of years. Many Sioux believe that their people have always lived on the land near the Black Hills in South Dakota. Other people think that the Sioux probably first lived in the woods of central Minnesota.

In the woodlands, the Sioux lived in small villages in homes made of bark. They traveled by canoe and on foot to catch fish, gather wild rice, and hunt. These early Sioux also grew corn.

Around A.D. 1500, the Sioux people split into three groups. The groups became known as the Lakota (or Teton), the Dakota (or Santee), and the Nakota (or Yankton and Yanktonai). Each group spoke the Sioux language differently. But they shared many traditions.

The Lakota, Dakota, and Nakota were further divided into seven smaller groups. These groups became the Seven Council Fires, or the Oceti Sakowin. Each summer, the Oceti Sakowin would come together for a ceremony. They also talked about things that were important to the Sioux nation.

Many early Sioux lived in the woods of central Minnesota around Lake Mille Lacs.

WHAT'S IN A NAME?

The name *Sioux* is not a Sioux word. It comes from the Ojibwe word *na-towe-ssiwa*. Over time, Europeans shortened the word to *Sioux*. When the U.S. government used this word for all Lakota, Dakota, and Nakota people, the name stuck. Most Sioux prefer to be called Lakota, Dakota, or Nakota. They say that these words mean "friend."

WIDE OPEN SPACES

The Sioux were not the only people living in the woodlands of Minnesota. Other American Indian tribes also lived on this rich land. Tribes such as the Ojibwe often battled with the Sioux. Many lives were lost. The Lakota and Nakota wanted to protect their people from war. They decided to leave the woods in the late 1600s or early 1700s. They headed west for the wide open spaces of the Great Plains. The Dakota stayed in Minnesota.

By 1720, the Nakota had settled on the grassy prairies of modern-day South Dakota and Iowa. They also came to live in parts of North Dakota. The Lakota traveled west of the Nakota. By the end of the 1700s, they lived on land near the Black Hills in South Dakota. They also lived in parts of modern-day Wisconsin, North Dakota, Montana, Wyoming, and Nebraska.

The Great Plains stretch from western Canada to southern Texas. Most of this area is grassland with few trees.

The Dakota remained in the woodlands of
Minnesota longer than the Lakota or Nakota.
There they kept many of their woodland
traditions. They lived in bark homes, grew corn,
and gathered wild rice.

The Dakota also began trading with French
trappers. These men had come from Europe to hunt
animals for their valuable fur. The French also
bought fur from Dakota hunters. They paid the
Dakota with European goods, such as guns, metal
tools, glass beads, and cloth.

The Dakota lived in bark houses. They hunted in the woods near their
homes. They fished and gathered wild rice in the rivers and lakes.

HORSES AND GUNS

The Sioux and other American Indians lived for hundreds of years without horses or guns. They traveled on foot. They used dogs to pull or carry their belongings. To hunt and fight battles, they used bows and arrows and other handmade weapons. Spanish explorers and settlers introduced horses and guns to the Americas. These two things changed the way the Sioux and other American Indians lived. Horses allowed the Sioux to travel much farther distances in shorter periods of time. Both horses and guns helped the Sioux hunt down buffalo and other land animals more easily. The Sioux also used guns and horses to win battles and claim more and more land.

LIFE WITH THE BUFFALO

On the plains, the Sioux adjusted to a new way of living. They no longer lived in villages. Instead, they traveled from place to place according to the seasons. They also began using horses to travel farther and faster. During the spring, summer, and fall, the Sioux followed herds of American bison, or buffalo.

These large animals were plentiful, and the Sioux became skilled buffalo hunters.

The buffalo provided the Sioux with almost everything they needed to survive. Buffalo meat gave them food. Fur and skin became warm clothing and material for homes. Bones were made into tools, weapons, and even sleds.

The Sioux had great respect for the buffalo. They tried to kill only as many animals as they needed to survive. They gave thanks to the buffalo before and after each hunt. They also made sure not to waste any part of the buffalo they killed.

Buffalo moved across the prairie and plains looking for enough wild grass to eat.

The Sioux used animal skins to make clothing such as moccasins. This pair is decorated with dyed porcupine quills and beads.

After a big hunt, the Sioux often had a feast. The women roasted some of the meat over a fire. Other times, they boiled the meat in hot water. After the feast, the women preserved the rest of the meat. They pounded the meat flat and let it harden and dry. The dried meat lasted many months.

Women also cleaned the skin, or hides, of the buffalo. They used these hides to make clothing for their families. They sewed warm robes, leggings, dresses, and shoes called moccasins.

Another important job of Sioux women was making tipis out of buffalo hides. Tipi homes were made of tall wooden poles. The poles came together at the top of the tipi to make a cone shape. Warm buffalo skins covered the outside of the tipi. Families decorated their tipis with artwork on the outside and inside walls.

The Sioux decorated their tipis with drawings.

Many Sioux lived in tipis for some or all of the year.

Inside the tipi, soft buffalo skins covered the floor. A warm fire helped make the tipi a cozy place during the bitterly cold winter months. In the hot summer, the flaps of the tipi could be rolled up to let air flow through. Tipis were also a perfect home for people on the move. They could be packed away and carried easily from place to place.

CHAPTER 2

FAMILY LIFE

THE SIOUX TRAVELED AND LIVED TOGETHER in groups called bands. The Dakota were divided into four bands. The Nakota formed two bands. And the Lakota had seven bands. The bands were made up of smaller family groups called *tiospayes*.

A tiospaye included several related families. Sometimes friends and distant relatives also joined a tiospaye. The leaders led the younger men in hunts. The leaders also led battles against enemy tribes. It was the job of the leaders to make sure that everyone in their tiospaye had enough to eat and was protected from danger.

The men and women in a tiospaye worked together to raise the children in their group. They passed on to the children the importance of bravery, strength, generosity, and wisdom.

This drawing shows a Sioux settlement in South Dakota. Families lived together to form communities.

This Sioux woman is wearing traditional clothing from the late 1800s.

Grandmothers, mothers, and aunts taught girls from a young age. Girls learned how to cook, gather wood for fires, collect water, and sew clothing. They also learned how to pick wild fruits and vegetables, such as berries and turnips.

When a girl began to grow into a young woman, her mother took her aside for a special ceremony. For four days, the daughter lived alone in a small tipi. The mother spent some of that time teaching her daughter the art of making moccasins and decorating with quills.

Grandfathers, fathers, and uncles taught young boys how to hunt and be warriors. The boys used small bows and arrows to hunt animals such as rabbits. Later, they were given larger bows to hunt deer, antelope, and eventually buffalo. The boys also learned the skill of fishing.

Around the age of eleven or twelve, many Sioux boys began their training to be warriors. They joined the men in battles, but they did not fight. At first, they simply served the warriors by bringing them food and water.

Sioux men hunted with spears, bows and arrows, and guns. In the winter, men often wore snowshoes. They helped the men chase animals across deep snow.

The shield was important to the Sioux. They used it for protection and for ceremonies.

FEARLESS FIGHTERS

Most boys were eager to prove their bravery in war. The Lakota prized this kind of bravery above all else. The Sioux always had to be alert for enemies. Other tribes often wanted to take over Sioux hunting grounds. The Sioux needed great courage to fight their toughest enemies. Many American Indian tribes feared and admired them. The Lakota were especially known as fearless fighters.

Before a battle, a Sioux warrior put on face paint. He often wore eagle feathers in his hair. The paint and feathers told the story of the warrior's brave deeds in past battles. During a battle, a warrior earned respect by risking his life to beat the enemy. Skillful Sioux fighters won many battles. This allowed them to take control of large pieces of land. Over time, they came to be one of the most powerful tribes on the Great Plains.

The bravest Lakota warriors, such as Black Rock *(right)*, wore a headdress made of eagle feathers and buffalo horns.

Dakota in Minnesota perform a traditional ceremony called the Medicine Dance in the 1840s.

SIOUX SPIRITUALITY

The Sioux often sang and chanted prayers to ask for success in war and in hunting. They also performed ceremonies to protect themselves and their families from danger and sickness.

The Sioux believed in one all-powerful spirit called Wakan Tanka. Wakan Tanka was also known as the Great Spirit. The Sioux believed Wakan Tanka was in every part of the universe in the form of less powerful spirits. Wakan Tanka was in the sun, the sky, and the winds. Wakan Tanka was also part of the animals in nature, such as the buffalo, the bear, and the eagle.

The biggest ceremony of the year was the Sun Dance. This ceremony happened each summer in late June or early July. It was a time for dances, prayer, and visiting with family and friends. It was also a time for people to pray to Wakan Tanka for good fortune.

Some men asked for power and wisdom from Wakan Tanka during the Sun Dance. These men fasted, or ate nothing, during the ceremony. They also danced for many hours. They believed this experience would help them feel the power of Wakan Tanka.

A Lakota man named Short Bull (1845–1915) painted this picture of the Sun Dance.

WHITE BUFFALO CALF WOMAN

During the Sun Dance and other ceremonies, the Sioux smoked a special pipe. Smoking the pipe helped the Sioux communicate with Wakan Tanka.

The Lakota say that a spirit called the White Buffalo Calf Woman gave their people the original pipe hundreds of years ago. She first appeared to two Lakota warriors hunting for buffalo. She wore clothing made of white buckskin and carried a wrapped bundle. The White Buffalo Calf Woman told the warriors she would bring their people a special gift. Four days later, she appeared to the Lakota people. She gave them the sacred pipe and told them how to use it. She also taught them how to live good lives and how to pray to Wakan Tanka.

Since then, the pipe has been passed down among the Lakota. In 1966, twelve-year-old Arvol Looking Horse became the nineteenth keeper of the sacred pipe.

Arvol Looking Horse in 2003

CHAPTER 3

NEW NEIGHBORS

THE LAKOTA AND NAKOTA MOSTLY LIVED APART from white people in the 1700s. At the same time, the Dakota continued to trade with white trappers and traders. By the 1760s, the British had taken over the woodlands from the French. Then American colonists won the American Revolution (1775–1783) against the British. The colonists formed a new nation, the United States of America.

Meriwether Lewis and William Clark *(center)* traveled through Sioux hunting grounds in 1804. The explorers were trying to map a route up the Missouri River to the Pacific Ocean.

In 1803, the French sold a large amount of land to U.S. president Thomas Jefferson. This land was known as the Louisiana Territory. It included the Great Plains, where the Sioux lived. White settlers began moving into this land west of the Mississippi River. They hoped to start a new life on the land of the Sioux and other Native Americans.

The Dakota's way of life was the first to be changed by the white settlers. The settlers hunted buffalo and other animals. After a while, there weren't enough animals left to hunt.

The settlers also cut down trees. They took over the best land to build homes, farms, and ranches. Soon the Dakota were struggling to survive.

TREATIES WITH THE U.S. GOVERNMENT

To protect part of their land, some Dakota leaders had to sign treaties with the U.S. government. Treaties are written agreements. In the treaties, the Sioux agreed to give up large amounts of their land. Instead, they would live on smaller pieces of land called reservations.

Fort Snelling *(below)* in Minnesota was built on land that the Dakota gave to the U.S. government in a treaty. The Dakota and other Indians often visited this military post to trade.

In exchange, the U.S. government was supposed to pay the Dakota for their land. The government agreed to provide them with food and supplies.

The Nakota and Lakota also started having problems with whites. Thousand of settlers had begun passing through Sioux land on their way west. Sometimes they decided to settle on parts of Sioux territory and claim it for themselves. At first, the Sioux were friendly with these white travelers. But the settlers could be greedy hunters.

Some settlers built houses on Sioux land. The houses in this photograph were built in the Black Hills in the 1800s.

This painting shows members of the Dakota and the U.S. government signing a treaty in 1851.

They killed too many buffalo. Many settlers also treated the Sioux as enemies. Some settlers even attacked and killed Sioux people.

To protect themselves, the Sioux began to fight back. The U.S. government wanted to stop these attacks. In 1851, it wrote another treaty. The treaty called for peace between U.S. citizens and American Indians living on the plains. But the treaty did not solve the problems. Fighting still broke out between the two sides. The U.S. government sent soldiers to protect the settlers. Battles between the Sioux and U.S. soldiers began to take place regularly.

THE REASON OF THE INDIAN OUTBREAK.
General Miles declares that the Indians are starved into rebellion.

White government officials were in charge of everything on reservations. This cartoon shows a dishonest official stealing from a starving Plains Indian.

THE SIOUX UPRISING OF 1862

The Dakota in Minnesota did not fight with their white neighbors. But they were not happy with life on the reservation. The food, money, and education the U.S. government had promised them often did not come. By the harsh winter of 1862, many Dakota were starving. Months went by. But the government failed to send the things they had agreed to give the Sioux. That summer, the Dakota lost their patience.

In August 1862, some Dakota made war on government officials and white settlers in the area. U.S. soldiers came to fight the Dakota. Hundreds of people on both sides died. This tragic event became known as the Sioux Uprising.

The U.S. government punished many Dakota who had taken part in the uprising. It hanged thirty-eight men. It sent about three hundred others to a prison camp in Iowa. The uprising and punishment of so many Sioux became a painful memory for the Dakota.

Thirty-eight Dakota men were hanged in Mankato, Minnesota, in 1862. It was the largest execution in U.S. history.

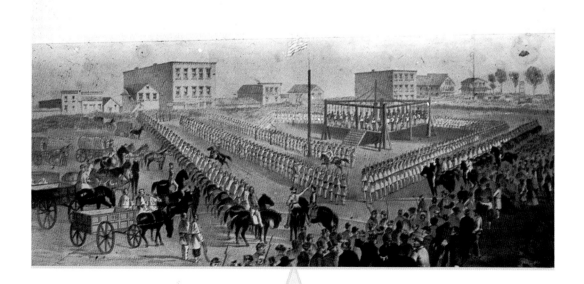

CHAPTER 4
WAR ON THE PLAINS

PROBLEMS BETWEEN THE U.S. GOVERNMENT and the Nakota and Lakota Sioux continued during the 1860s. A Lakota leader named Red Cloud decided to fight back. In 1866, he led his fighters and other American Indians in a major war against U.S. soldiers. Their goal was to protect Native American lands in modern-day Wyoming and Montana.

The Lakota won this war. But Red Cloud knew that more deadly battles would come. He chose peace instead. In 1868, he and other Lakota leaders signed the Fort Laramie Treaty. They agreed to move to a reservation on the western half of South Dakota. This land included the sacred Black Hills. In return, the U.S. government promised the Lakota that the Black Hills would always belong to them.

BUFFALO KILLINGS

In the late 1860s, the U.S. government hired white hunters to kill off buffalo on the plains. At first, the buffalo were killed because of the new railroad across the United States. Buffalo could cause accidents if they moved in front of trains. Settlers also wanted to make room for farms, cattle ranches, and homes. After a while, the U.S. government realized that killing off the buffalo weakened the Sioux and other Plains Indians. That gave the government a new reason to remove these animals from the land. By the end of the 1800s, millions of buffalo had been killed. Fewer than one thousand buffalo roamed the plains.

Miners search for gold in the Dakota Territory in 1876.

LITTLE BIGHORN

In the early 1870s, gold was discovered in the Black Hills. Thousands of people rushed there. They hoped to find gold and become rich. The U.S. government did not stop people from going onto Lakota land in search of gold. Instead, the government tried to buy the Black Hills from the Lakota. But Red Cloud and other leaders said that the Black Hills were not for sale. They would not leave the area.

In 1876, the U.S. government decided to force all Sioux away from the Black Hills and onto reservations. Some Lakota went to the reservations. Many others refused. They did not want the U.S. government to tell them where to live. Reservations were often small. The people who lived on them did not have the freedom to travel and hunt on the Great Plains.

U.S. soldiers tried to hunt down all the Lakota. "Wherever we went, soldiers came to kill us," remembered a Lakota Sioux named Black Elk.

Sioux on a reservation in South Dakota wait to receive beef from the U.S. government.

The Sioux fought back to protect their freedom. Two powerful Lakota leaders led this fight. They were called Sitting Bull and Crazy Horse.

In June 1876, U.S. Lieutenant Colonel George Armstrong Custer attacked a large village of Sioux, Cheyenne, and Arapaho Indians. The village sat along the Little Bighorn River in Montana. Sitting Bull, Crazy Horse, and other Indian leaders led the fight against Custer. Custer's army was no match for them. He and all of his soldiers died in the battle.

Sitting Bull was a great spiritual leader. His visions and his courage made him a feared enemy of the U.S. government.

A Lakota named Kicking Bear (1846–1904) painted this picture of the Battle of the Little Bighorn. He is one of the men standing in the center.

The Battle of the Little Bighorn was an important victory for the Sioux. It showed the U.S. government that the Sioux were determined to keep their land. But the battle also added to the fears of U.S. citizens. Most of them did not understand or respect the Sioux and other American Indians. They thought Native Americans were cruel and wild. Many people wanted all Native Americans to live on reservations away from U.S. citizens.

Fighting between the Sioux and U.S. soldiers continued. The U.S. government was determined to chase down all the Sioux and force them onto reservations. In 1877, Crazy Horse finally surrendered. Sitting Bull and his followers fled to safety in Canada. Some of these Sioux stayed in Canada. Sitting Bull returned to his homeland in 1881 and agreed to live on a reservation.

CRAZY HORSE (ca. 1840–1877), or Tasunka Witco, was a highly respected Lakota leader and warrior. He wanted to defend the traditions and values of the Lakota way of life. To protect Lakota lands and freedom, he fought many battles against white soldiers. One of the most famous was the Battle of the Little Bighorn. In 1877, the U.S. government made a promise to Crazy Horse. If he would surrender, he and his family would be placed on their own reservation. He agreed and was brought to the Red Cloud Agency in Nebraska. Soon after, the government tried to arrest him. Crazy Horse attempted to get away but was killed in the struggle.

The Sioux were forced to live on reservations. Many of their customs and ceremonies were not allowed there. The Sioux were taught to act and dress like white people instead.

WOUNDED KNEE

By the 1880s, most Lakota, Nakota, and Dakota people lived on reservations. There, white officials tried to change the Sioux. The U.S. government wanted American Indians to give up their old ways of life. On reservations, the Sioux were not allowed to have traditional dances and other ceremonies. They could not roam and hunt freely. And their leaders had very little power. The U.S. government hoped these rules would force the Sioux to become more like white citizens.

American Indian children work at a chalkboard under a teacher's watchful eye. The teachers were usually European Americans.

The government made many Sioux children attend boarding schools miles away. The children lived at these schools. They received English names, clothing, and haircuts. Teachers would severely punish American Indian children for speaking their own language. Many lost touch with their history and traditions.

Many Sioux longed for the old days of freedom and community. In the late 1880s, some of them began practicing a new ceremony called the Ghost Dance. They believed that the Ghost Dance would help them return to life before Europeans came.

The U.S. government worried that members of the new movement might try to fight for their freedom. Government officers arrested Sioux leaders who followed the Ghost Dance. On December 15, 1890, they arrested Sitting Bull. During a struggle after his arrest, an officer killed him.

After that, followers of Sitting Bull and other Sioux leaders fled the area. Some of them made camp along Wounded Knee Creek in South Dakota. On December 29, U.S. soldiers attacked the camp. They killed at least 150 Sioux men, women, and children. This tragic event became known as the Wounded Knee Massacre.

A group of Native Americans form a circle around the people performing the Ghost Dance.

CHAPTER 5

BUILDING A FUTURE

AFTER THE WOUNDED KNEE MASSACRE, many Sioux felt defeated and hopeless. Reservation life continued to be very hard. In 1934, a law was passed that returned some rights to American Indians. The law gave them the right to form their own governments. It also gave money to American Indians to make life better on reservations.

For a while, life did get better for Sioux and Native Americans on reservations. But these changes did not last. By the 1950s, the U.S. government stopped helping Native Americans on reservations. Many young people started new lives in towns and cities.

CHARLES EASTMAN (1858–1939), or Ohiyesa, was raised as a traditional Dakota. He became a doctor, a writer, and a naturalist at a time when the Sioux people struggled against unfair treatment in the United States. He was a spokesperson for the Sioux people and fought hard for his people's rights. He worked to educate Sioux children. He also helped build the Boy Scouts of America.

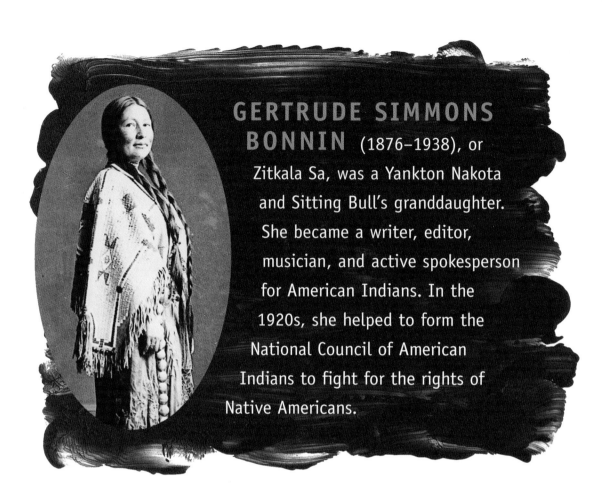

GERTRUDE SIMMONS BONNIN (1876–1938), or Zitkala Sa, was a Yankton Nakota and Sitting Bull's granddaughter. She became a writer, editor, musician, and active spokesperson for American Indians. In the 1920s, she helped to form the National Council of American Indians to fight for the rights of Native Americans.

SPEAKING OUT

In 1968, Sioux and other Native American leaders organized the American Indian Movement (AIM). Members of AIM spoke out for the rights of Native Americans. They believed in the ability of American Indian communities to take care of themselves. AIM also wanted Native Americans to take pride in the spirituality and values of their traditional culture.

Members of AIM led many protests to speak out against poor treatment. In 1973, they led a protest at Wounded Knee, on a Lakota reservation. The protesters stayed at Wounded Knee for seventy-one days. This and other protests helped bring about important changes.

Beginning in the 1970s, the U.S. government passed laws to support schools, medical clinics, and housing programs run by American Indians.

A member of the American Indian Movement offers a pipe to the assistant U.S. attorney general, ending the protest at Wounded Knee.

Other laws protected the right of American Indians to freely practice their traditions and spiritual beliefs. The U.S. government also began to return some land it had taken from American Indians in the past.

MODERN LIFE

At least 150,000 Sioux live in the United States. Many of these Lakota, Nakota, and Dakota people have worked hard to create a better life on reservations. They have built schools and colleges to teach young people tribal languages, history, and customs. They have opened community centers.

THE BLACK HILLS

In 1980, the U.S. government offered to pay the Sioux more than $100 million for some of the land they had lost. But the Sioux refused to take the money. Instead, they asked for the Black Hills to be returned to them. The U.S. government said no to this request. The Sioux continue to fight for the right to claim this land.

These Sioux children play in a field near
their home in South Dakota.

And they have strengthened their own tribal
governments. These governments include elected
leaders who make decisions for each reservation.
The leaders also speak out on behalf of their
community.

Many Sioux take pride in their communities on
the reservations. They have turned reservation
lands into true homes. Modern Sioux reservations
are in North Dakota, South Dakota, Minnesota,
Montana, Nebraska, and Canada.

Poverty and unemployment are still problems for some reservation members. Some people do not have the education or skills needed for well-paying jobs. And there are not always enough jobs for everyone on a reservation. But many people work as farmers, cattle ranchers, teachers, doctors, police officers, or tribal government workers. Some reservations also own and operate casinos. The casinos provide jobs for Sioux people and for people in nearby communities.

Sioux who live on and off reservations come together in the summer months to celebrate their traditions. *Wacipis*, or powwows, are traditional

Sioux people have all sorts of jobs. This woman is a police officer.

People who take part in dancing contests at wacipis often wear brightly colored traditional clothing.

summer gatherings. They usually last from two to four days. Big wacipis draw hundreds of people from all over the country. Traditional dancing is an important part of wacipis. People can also join in rodeos, races, and other games.

Some families host special celebrations called giveaways during wacipis. Giveaways are often held after someone has died. They also honor people who have reached a goal, such as graduating from high school. The host family gives gifts to people who helped the person being honored.

The Heritage Center at Red Cloud Indian School displays some of the best artwork from past Red Cloud Indian Art Shows.

Each June through August, the Red Cloud Indian Art Show takes place. It is held at the Pine Ridge Indian Reservation in South Dakota. Native American artists from anywhere in North America can show their artwork. They enter paintings, sculptures, and other artwork in this competition. Prizes are awarded for the best pieces of art. Visitors and art collectors from across the United States and from many foreign countries come to the show each year.

The Crazy Horse Memorial is an important piece of art for some Sioux. This giant sculpture is being carved out of the Black Hills of South Dakota near Mount Rushmore. More than sixty years ago, the faces of four U.S. presidents were carved into Mount Rushmore.

Some Sioux were unhappy that these sculptures of white leaders were made in the Black Hills. They decided to create their own sculpture. They wanted to honor a great Lakota hero and the bravery of the Sioux people. But many Sioux are not happy with this sculpture either. They do not think it is right for anyone to carve into the sacred Black Hills.

The Crazy Horse Memorial will show the leader and warrior proudly riding his horse. When it is finished, the entire sculpture will be 641 feet long and 563 feet high.

The Sioux have faced many challenges in their long history. They have overcome difficult times. They continue to strengthen their communities and to preserve and celebrate their culture. They are meeting the future while honoring their past.

Nakota brothers Mato Nanji *(left)* and Ptehcaka Wicasa play their guitars. They and other family members formed a successful blues-rock band called Indigenous.

FRY BREAD

This deep-fried bread is a traditional Lakota treat served at wacipis and other gatherings.

1 cup lukewarm water	*1 teaspoon salt*
1 package yeast	*4 cups flour*
2 tablespoons shortening	*vegetable oil*
1 tablespoon sugar	

1. Put water and yeast in large bowl. Stir.
2. Wait 5 minutes. Stir in shortening, sugar, and salt.
3. Combine with 2 cups flour. Add 2 more cups flour and mix with your hands.
4. Spread light layer of flour on counter or table. Place dough on it. Knead dough with your hands.
5. Coat inside of clean bowl with vegetable oil. Place kneaded dough in bowl and let rise for 1 hour.
6. Pinch off golf-ball-sized pieces of dough and stretch into flat circles. Make small cut in middle of each circle.
7. Heat 1 to 2 inches of vegetable oil in a frying pan. (Do not touch hot cooking oil.)
8. Place dough in pan. Fry until bottom side is brown. Flip over and cook other side until brown.
9. Take out of pan and place on paper towels.

Enjoy!

PLACES TO VISIT

Akta Lakota Museum
Chamberlin, SD
800-798-3452
http://www.aktalakota.org/
The Akta Lakota Musuem, whose name means "to honor the people," is open to anyone interested in learning more about the Lakota people. It also displays work by Lakota artists and craftspeople.

The Crazy Horse Memorial
Crazy Horse, South Dakota
(605) 673-4681
http://www.crazyhorse.org/
This in-progress memorial to the famous Lakota leader and warrior is open to visitors, along with an Indian museum and cultural center.

The Heritage Center
Pine Ridge, South Dakota
(605) 867-5491
http://www.redcloudschool.org/museum/museum.htm
Located on the Lakota Sioux Pine Ridge Indian Reservation, this museum and cultural resource center contains historical exhibits and a collection of award-winning Indian art.

Pipestone National Monument
Pipestone, Minnesota
(507) 825-5464
http://www.nps.gov/pipe/
This national park preserves the traditional rock quarries that the Sioux visited to make pipes and other sacred items. It includes a cultural center and a trail through native prairie to the pipestone quarries.

GLOSSARY

band: a group of American Indians that live and travel together. A band is usually part of a larger group, such as a tribe.

giveaway: the giving of gifts to many people in honor of someone

Great Plains: a strip of treeless land in central North America that stretches thousands of miles from Canada to Texas

Oceti Sakowin (oh-CHAY-tee shah-KOH-ween): the Seven Council Fires, or seven major divisions of the Great Sioux Nation. There are four Dakota bands, two Nakota bands, and the Lakota. The seven Lakota bands form another Seven Council Fires.

reservation: an area of land set aside by the U.S. government for a particular American Indian group. Most Indians were forced off their homeland and onto reservations in the 1800s.

territory: an area of land that is part of another country or controlled by that country's government

tiospayes (tih-OHS-pa-yays): small groups of American Indians that are made up of several related families and their close friends

tipis: cone-shaped homes made of tall wooden poles and covered with animal skins

treaty: a written agreement between two or more nations or groups

tribe: a group of American Indians who share the same language, customs, and beliefs. Modern Sioux tribe members are usually from the same reservation.

wacipis (wah-CHEE-pees): powwows, or summer gatherings, that often last several days. These celebrations feature traditional dancing and music. They can also include rodeos, races, and games.

Wakan Tanka (wah-KAHN TAHN-kah): the Great Spirit. Wakan Tanka is the creator and part of everything sacred to the Sioux.

FURTHER READING

Aller, Susan Bivin. *Sitting Bull*. Minneapolis: Lerner Publications Company, 2004. This is a biography of the famous Lakota Sioux leader and warrior.

Birchfield, D. L. *Crazy Horse*. Austin, TX: Raintree Steck-Vaughn, 2003. This book is a biography of Crazy Horse, a Lakota Sioux hero.

Braine, Susan. *Drumbeat . . . Heartbeat: A Celebration of the Powwow*. Minneapolis: Lerner Publications Company, 1995. Braine offers an inside look at the preparation and celebration of a Northern Plains powwow.

Goble, Paul. *The Legend of the White Buffalo Woman*. Washington, DC: National Geographic Society, 1998. Beautiful paintings and prose retell the story of how the Lakota met the White Buffalo Calf Woman.

Isaacs, Sally Senzell. *Life in a Sioux Village*. Chicago: Heinemann Library, 2002. Isaacs describes the daily life of a Plains Sioux band before modern times.

Kavasch, E. Barrie. *Lakota Sioux Children and Elders Talk Together*. New York: PowerKids Press, 1999. A young girl and several elders talk about the land, culture, traditions, and modern life of Lakota Sioux on the Pine Ridge Indian Reservation in South Dakota.

Littlefield, Holly. *Children of the Indian Boarding Schools*. Minneapolis: Carolrhoda Books, Inc., 2001. The author describes the experiences of American Indian children who lived in boarding schools.

WEBSITES

Black Hills & Badlands: The Great Sioux Nation
http://www.blackhillsbadlands.com/go.asp?ID=102
This website includes a description of the Lakota Sioux and informative links to three Lakota reservations in the area.

Dakota Society Tutorial
http://www.visi.com/~vanmulken/Tutorial/intro.html
This informative website of the Dakota Society of Minnesota includes a
children's tutorial link with facts and quizzes about the Dakota Sioux.

Minnesota Indian Affairs Council
http://www.cri-bsu.org/IA_web/htdocs/tribes/
The council's website provides information on Minnesota's Dakota
Sioux reservations: Shakopee Mdewakanton, Prairie Island, Lower
Sioux, and Upper Sioux.

SELECTED BIBLIOGRAPHY

Calloway, Collin G., ed. *Our Hearts Fell to the Ground: Plains Indians
Views of How the West Was Lost*. Boston: Bedford Books, 1996.

Gibbon, Guy. *The Sioux: The Dakota and Lakota Nations*. Malden, MA:
Blackwell Publishing, 2003.

Hassrick, Royal B. *The Sioux: Life and Customs of a Warrior Society*.
Norman: University of Oklahoma Press, 1964.

Iverson, Peter, ed. *The Plains Indians of the Twentieth Century*. Norman:
University of Oklahoma Press, 1985.

Robinson, Doane. *Dakota or Sioux Indians*. Minneapolis: Ross & Haines,
Inc, 1904.

Rosenfelt, Willard E. *The Last Buffalo. Cultural Views of the Plains Indians:
The Sioux or Dakota Nation*. Minneapolis: T. S. Denison & Co., 1973.

Sandoz, Mari. *These Were the Sioux*. Lincoln: University of Nebraska Press,
1985.

INDEX